Original title:
The Fading Light

Copyright © 2024 Creative Arts Management OÜ
All rights reserved.

Author: Robert Ashford
ISBN HARDBACK: 978-9916-90-092-5
ISBN PAPERBACK: 978-9916-90-093-2

Glowing Afterthought

In the quiet night, stars softly gleam,
Whispers of dreams float through the stream.
Shadows dance lightly, secrets unfold,
Memories linger, stories retold.

Through the calm air, a breeze draws near,
Carrying echoes of laughter and cheer.
Time drips slowly, painting the skies,
Fading moments, where silence lies.

Upon the horizon, dawn begins to rise,
Illuminating thoughts, like fireflies.
Each glowing spark, a fragment of light,
Guiding the heart through the deepening night.

In this embrace, from dusk to dawn,
We hold onto dreams that are never gone.
Each afterthought glows, a guiding star,
Reminding us always, just who we are.

Last Glimmers

The sun dips low, a soft goodbye,
Colors dance across the sky.
Whispers wrap around the breeze,
Nature sighs with gentle ease.

Shadows stretch as daylight fades,
Links of gold in twilight's shades.
Stars awaken, twinkling bright,
Heralding the coming night.

When Day Meets Night

A canvas brushed with crimson hue,
Where day and night begin to brew.
The horizon blurs, a fleeting line,
In the embrace of dusk, divine.

Silent wonders softly call,
As evening blankets one and all.
Time does pause, it holds its breath,
In this moment, life feels death.

Flickering Reverie

Memories dance like candlelight,
Fleeting notes in endless night.
Each flicker tells a story old,
In whispers of the brave and bold.

Dreams awaken, shadows play,
In the twilight, colors sway.
A world of wonder comes alive,
In the dusk where hopes survive.

Embrace of the Dusk

The stars emerge, a velvet sheet,
In the stillness, hearts do meet.
Time wraps us in its gentle fold,
As mysteries of night unfold.

With every breath, the shadows creep,
Dancing secrets, soft and deep.
In the embrace of fading light,
We find solace in the night.

Lingering Glow

In twilight's tender hold, they dance,
Fading sunlight, a fleeting chance.
Colors merge, a soft embrace,
Whispers of day, now out of place.

Stars begin their gentle rise,
Painting dreams across the skies.
Night breathes deep, in shadows grow,
Holding tight to lingering glow.

Murmurs of Nightfall

The moon spills silver on the stream,
While crickets hum a twilight dream.
Soft breezes speak in hushed tones,
As nature sings to twilight's moans.

Wisps of fog creep, weaving slow,
Embracing earth in gentle flow.
Murmurs whisper through the trees,
Carried softly by the breeze.

Glorious Disappearance

As daylight wanes to dusky hues,
The world unwinds, a gentle muse.
Mountains fade, horizons blend,
In this magic, all hearts mend.

The sun bows low, its curtain calls,
Casting shadows on ancient walls.
Moments linger, then take flight,
In the glorious turn of night.

The Quietude of Dusk

When day concedes to night's embrace,
Finding peace in this still space.
Softly drapes the fading light,
A tranquil pause, from day to night.

Whispers linger, soft and low,
In the quietude, time moves slow.
Hearts entwined, as natures sighs,
Underneath the starry skies.

Veil of Coming Night

Soft whispers float through the trees,
As daylight fades to a gentle tease.
Stars peek through the fabric of sky,
Embracing the hush of the night nearby.

Shadows lengthen and softly creep,
Inviting dreams from the depths of sleep.
Moonlight dances on dew-kissed ground,
In the silence, peace can be found.

Silhouettes in Sinking Sun

Golden hues stain the horizon wide,
Where nature's wonders take their stride.
Figures emerge in a radiant glow,
As daylight bows and begins to slow.

Birds take flight in a fervent rush,
Against the canvas that glows and blushes.
Each silhouette tells a tale untold,
In this fleeting moment, pure and bold.

Threads of Gloaming Grace

Weaving shadows in twilight's embrace,
Threads of light start to interlace.
Crickets serenade the waiting night,
As dusk drapes the world in soft twilight.

Whispers of lore in the cool evening air,
Hold secrets that linger without a care.
Time slows down as the stars come alive,
In the tender glow where memories thrive.

When Day Meets Night

A horizon split in a dance of light,
Where day meets night in a radiant sight.
Colors swirl in a breathtaking display,
Celebrating endings, blessing the day.

The sun bows low, bidding farewell,
While shadows rise from their quiet shell.
In this moment, all worlds align,
As dusk unfolds, with every sign.

A Soft Goodbye

Whispers linger in the air,
Tears glisten with a quiet flare.
Promises spoken, hearts entwined,
In the silence, love defined.

Footsteps fade on the dampened ground,
Hope and sorrow tightly bound.
Time stands still as shadows play,
In the dusk, we softly sway.

Memories dance within the light,
Pulling softly on the night.
In the stillness, sparks ignite,
A soft goodbye feels just right.

The Golden Hour's Last Breath

The sun dips low, a gentle sigh,
Painting skies as day waves goodbye.
Golden rays that softly gleam,
Mingle with the evening's dream.

Whispers of warmth in the cool air,
As shadows stretch with tender care.
The horizon glows, a fleeting sight,
Holding tight to the fading light.

Time slows down in this embrace,
Nature's canvas, a breathtaking grace.
The last breath lingers, bold and bright,
In the arms of the coming night.

Silencing Brilliance

Stars above in endless night,
Twinkling tales of hidden light.
Yet silence wraps each shimmering spark,
Hiding stories in the dark.

Each glow a secret, softly spun,
Echoes of worlds no longer run.
In the quiet, their brilliance fades,
Mysteries lost in the shadowed shades.

A luminous dance, now at rest,
Dreams adorn the celestial vest.
In their silence, whispers plead,
To reveal the truths we need.

The Last Breath of Day

As twilight wraps the world in peace,
The day exhales, its wonders cease.
Colors bleed into shades of gray,
A canvas shifting, night at play.

Birds retreat to nests they built,
A gentle calm, devoid of guilt.
Each rustle carries a soft refrain,
In the hush, we're left to gain.

The final glow begins to fade,
As dreams emerge from daylight's shade.
In the darkness, hopes emerge,
The last breath of day, a sacred surge.

Chasing the Dwindling Glow

In twilight's kiss, we run so free,
The fading light, a mystery.
We grasp for hope in shadows cast,
As daylight fades, the night holds fast.

The colors blend, a painter's dream,
A whispered prayer, a silken theme.
We chase the glow, though time may steal,
The warmth of rays that we can feel.

Stars awaken, bold and bright,
In the embrace of creeping night.
Yet in our hearts, the glow survives,
A cherished flame, where love thrives.

With every step, we forge our path,
Into the dark, we feel its wrath.
Yet still we run, come what may,
Chasing the dusk, by night we sway.

Silent Echoes of Dusk

As day retreats, the silence swells,
In evening's arms, soft magic dwells.
The whispers of the fading light,
Tell tales of dreams that grace the night.

The shadows stretch, they softly creep,
Where secrets nestled close, they sleep.
A breeze that hums an ancient tune,
As night unveils the silver moon.

In every sigh, there's history,
A song of dusk, a symphony.
The world in peace, it holds its breath,
In stillness found, there's life in death.

Embrace the dark, let silence reign,
In echo's fold, feel joy and pain.
For in the dusk, we brave the deep,
And in the still, our souls do leap.

Nightfall's Tender Caress

As night descends with gentle grace,
It wraps the world in a soft embrace.
The stars emerge, like diamonds bright,
In velvet skies, they dance with light.

The moonlight spills, a silver stream,
Awakening our secret dreams.
Each breath of night, a sweet caress,
In shadows deep, our hearts confess.

The world transforms, a mystic place,
As darkness weaves a lacy lace.
Each rustling leaf, a whispered tale,
The magic of the night prevails.

So let us roam in evening's glow,
Where time stands still, and spirits flow.
In nightfall's arms, we find our rest,
Embraced by dreams, forever blessed.

Hushed Tones of Retreating Day

With every shade, the daylight wanes,
In tranquil hues, the evening gains.
A palette drawn from sunlit rays,
That fades to soft, enchanting grays.

The chirping crickets take their place,
In nature's choir, a dulcet space.
The sky adorned in twilight's thread,
As whispers float where dreams are fed.

The pastel clouds, they drift away,
To make room for the starlit sway.
Each moment held in perfect tune,
In the hush of dusk, beneath the moon.

The day departs, yet love remains,
In every heartbeat, joy and pains.
We gather close, in shadows play,
Embracing life, the fading day.

Serenity in Shadows

In the hush of the night, soft whispers flow,
Gentle breezes dance, where the river will go.
Shadows wrap the earth, a calming embrace,
Finding peace in the dark, a cherished space.

Moonlight spills silver, illuminating each leaf,
Dreams take flight, weaving stories of grief.
Stars play the violin, tuning hearts to their song,
In this tranquil realm, we all belong.

The Last Brushstroke of Daylight

The sun dips low, painting skies in gold,
Embers of warmth, in soft hues unfold.
Clouds blush in shades of crimson and pink,
As twilight whispers, inviting us to think.

Colors blend gently, the canvas of night,
A final brushstroke, fading from sight.
As day bids farewell, in a tapestry spun,
We savor the stillness, the day finally done.

Whispered Secrets of the Twilight

Twilight descends, a soft cloak of peace,
Secrets are shared, as worries release.
Crickets begin their symphony's song,
Echoing mysteries where shadows belong.

Stars twinkle above, like eyes in the veil,
Tales of the night, from the moon they unveil.
In this gentle pause, the world feels alive,
In whispered secrets, our spirits will thrive.

.

Flickers of Time's Passage

Moments drift by, like leaves in the stream,
Fleeting and fragile, they vanish, it seems.
Time flickers softly, a candle's dim glow,
In each cherished heartbeat, life starts to show.

Memories linger, in shadows they play,
Echoes of laughter, guiding our way.
As dawn breaks anew, with a fresh breath we rise,
Embracing each flicker, beneath endless skies.

Vanishing Ember

In the hearth a flicker glows,
A warmth that whispers, then it goes.
Fleeting light in twilight's hand,
Time slips through like fine gran sand.

Memories dance in fading heat,
Echoing whispers of past feet.
Once bright flames now dwindling small,
Silent shadows start to crawl.

Night descends, the fire wanes,
Tales of old carried in the rains.
Each spark a moment lost in flight,
Leaving only soft, dark night.

Embers whisper secrets low,
In the dark, their stories flow.
Yet in silence, dreams still burn,
For every loss, a new return.

Shadows at Sundown

Golden rays begin to fade,
Casting shapes in twilight's glade.
Whispers linger, soft and clear,
As shadows stretch, drawing near.

Trees stand tall in still embrace,
Fingers reach for night's cool face.
The sky blushes with colors bright,
Bidding farewell to the light.

As day yields to evening's call,
Nighttime wraps around us all.
Footsteps muffled on the ground,
In this hush, peace is found.

Stars emerge, a distant light,
Guiding dreams into the night.
In shadows deep, we find our way,
Embracing darkness, come what may.

Before Night Falls

Hues of orange, pink, and red,
Paint the sky where daylight bled.
Last glimmers on the horizon's edge,
Whispers promise, a gentle pledge.

Birds take flight, the day does wane,
Nature holds its breath in vain.
A breeze carries sweet, soft sighs,
As the sun bids warm goodbyes.

Time stands still in this brief hour,
Softening light, a fleeting power.
Moments suspended in twilight's grace,
The world wrapped in a soft embrace.

As shadows stretch and night takes hold,
Stories linger, waiting to be told.
Before the stars greet the call,
We cherish the glow, before night falls.

Reflections in Dimming Glow

The day surrenders to the night,
A canvas washed in fading light.
Memories twinkle like stars above,
In mirrored pools of whispered love.

The last rays dance on river's crest,\nA tranquil heart seeks quiet rest.
With every ripple, stories flow,
In reflections of a dimming glow.

As darkness wraps the world around,
Echoes of laughter can still be found.
The heart remembers what is true,
In shadows cast, it dreams anew.

When stars ignite the evening air,
Hope ignites, a glowing flare.
For in each end, a start will grow,
In reflections of the dimming glow.

Glimmers of Memory

In whispers of the past, we find,
Fleeting shadows, small and kind.
The laughter echoes, softly clear,
Fragments of love still linger here.

Time-touched images swirl and glow,
A dance of ages, ebb and flow.
Each moment tethered, tightly bound,
In the depths of heart, they're found.

Faded letters, worn and frail,
Tell of journeys, hopes that sail.
Through tangled paths of joy and pain,
Glimmers of memory still remain.

As seasons change and years drift by,
We hold close what will never die.
In tender corners of the mind,
Infinite treasures we shall find.

Celestial Twilight

In the hush of twilight's glow,
Stars begin their evening show.
Silhouettes of trees stand tall,
Guardians hearing evening's call.

The sky painted in shades of blue,
Whispers of night come into view.
Breezes carry secrets old,
As dreams awaken, hearts unfold.

Moonbeams dance on silver streams,
Casting light on woven dreams.
Time slows down, a sacred space,
In twilight's arms, we find our grace.

Celestial wonders fill the night,
Guiding souls with gentle light.
In this moment, we transcend,
As day and night begin to blend.

Shadows Dancing

In the twilight, shadows creep,
Silent whispers start to leap.
Figures sway to a hidden tune,
Underneath the watchful moon.

Ghosts of dreams take gentle flight,
Weaving through the velvet night.
With every movement, tales unfold,
Secrets of the brave and bold.

In the corners, echoes play,
Lost in time, they sway and stay.
Memories linger, soft and bright,
In the shadows, dancing light.

With every turn, a story spun,
In the dark, we all are one.
Together in this fleeting trance,
We find our joy in shadows' dance.

When Glories Dim

When glories dim and fade away,
In gentle dusk, we learn to stay.
Lost in time's relentless flow,
We gather strength from what we know.

In quiet corners, whispers sigh,
Memories linger, never die.
With every end, a whispered start,
Rebirth blooms within the heart.

The echoes fade, yet still they call,
To rise again, to break the fall.
In twilight's grasp, we find our place,
When glories dim, we seek embrace.

Through shadows deep and valleys low,
Resilient spirits learn to grow.
For in the stillness, hope will gleam,
When glories dim, we dare to dream.

Footsteps in Twilight

Soft whispers call the night,
Beneath the fading light.
Shadows dance in gentle sway,
As dusk embraces day.

Lost in thoughts, we wander slow,
Where secret pathways glow.
Each step a story, worn and old,
In twilight's grasp, we are bold.

The stars begin to shine so bright,
Guiding us through this soft night.
Underneath the vast, dark sea,
Footsteps echo, wild and free.

Fleeting Mirage of Daylight

Fleeting rays in golden hue,
Chasing shadows, fleeting too.
In a blink, the magic fades,
Sunset strokes the evening shades.

Moments slip like grains of sand,
In the light, we take a stand.
Echoes of the day gone by,
As the dusk begins to sigh.

Time is but a fleeting friend,
With each sunset, we pretend.
Wishing moments would not flee,
But daylight's mirage will be free.

Dimmed Dreams

As night unfolds its quiet hand,
Whispers drift like grains of sand.
Hopes once bright now softly fade,
In the night's gentle cascade.

We gather dreams, though dimmed and small,
In the shadows, we hear their call.
Laughter lingers in the air,
A reminder, dreams still dare.

Softly, memories intertwine,
Through the dark, our spirits shine.
In quietude, we learn to find,
The beauty left in dreams unlined.

The Final Draw of Light

In the stillness, night takes hold,
As the day turns to ash and gold.
The sun dips low, a silent plea,
Leaving trails of memory.

With a final breath, it fades away,
Painting skies in shades of gray.
Promises made in light's embrace,
Now linger in this sacred space.

The stars begin their gentle climb,
While shadows dance to silent rhyme.
In the hush, the world feels right,
As we bid farewell to light.

Evening's Lament

The sun descends, a crimson sigh,
Whispers of day begin to die.
Stars awaken, shyly gleam,
Echoes of dusk, a fading dream.

The breeze recalls a tender tune,
As darkness calls the silver moon.
Soft shadows dance on twilight's stage,
A bittersweet farewell, the day's last page.

Crickets croon in soft delight,
Fading warmth of fading light.
Each breath a sigh, a gentle plea,
As night unveils its mystery.

Yet in this sorrow, hope does bloom,
For every night shall yield a room.
Where dreams reside, and wishes fly,
Beneath the vast and starry sky.

Silhouettes in the Gloaming

Figures dance in twilight's embrace,
Stretched shadows weave with grace.
Beneath the trees, a quiet sigh,
Time drifts slowly, like the sky.

The air is thick with whispered lore,
Of longing hearts and tales of yore.
Footsteps light on softening ground,
In the gloaming, magic's found.

A fleeting glance, a knowing smile,
Each moment savored, spent awhile.
As night approaches, spirits rise,
In the stillness, love never dies.

With every breath, the world will pause,
Celebrating nature's cause.
In shadows long, our stories twine,
Forever etched in hearts' design.

Hues of Approaching Night

Brushstrokes paint the evening sky,
Shades of orange, pink, and shy.
Clouds embrace the fading hue,
As daylight bids its last adieu.

Mountains wear a dusky veil,
In twilight's grip, the night prevails.
Softly, stars begin to blink,
In the silence, time will think.

A gentle hush, the world slows down,
As night holds court in its dark gown.
Dreams entwined with starlit skies,
In the quiet, hope still lies.

The colors blend, a canvas wide,
A tapestry where secrets hide.
Soon, the moon will take its flight,
Guiding souls through endless night.

Shadows Lengthen

As sun dips low, the shadows grow,
Glistening fields in softened glow.
Each shape entwined, a fleeting trace,
Whispers of time, a soft embrace.

Birds retreat to nests above,
In the quiet, stillness dove.
Leaves rustle with the evening's breath,
A gentle hush, a dance with death.

Crickets sing their evening song,
In the dark, where dreams belong.
Stars unveil their sparkling might,
In every corner, pure delight.

Though shadows lengthen, hearts will spark,
In the deepening, dwell the dark.
For in the night, a promise lies,
To awaken with the dawn's bright eyes.

Embrace of the Vanishing Sun

The sun dips low, a fiery glow,
Gentle whispers brush the meadow.
Shadows lengthen, dance and play,
In the embrace of the end of day.

Colors blend, a masterpiece,
Golden hues begin to cease.
A tranquil sigh, the world slows down,
As night prepares her velvet gown.

Birds take flight, their song retains,
A fleeting moment, joy sustains.
Nature holds her breath in awe,
In the twilight's soft, warm draw.

With every fade, a promise stays,
The sun's return in vibrant rays.
For in this moment, still and rare,
Life's beauty lingers in the air.

Linger of the Becoming Dark

Night unfurls her cloak of stars,
A tranquil peace, with no more scars.
The moon ascends, a silver guide,
In the quiet where dreams abide.

Faint shadows weave among the trees,
Softly swaying in the breeze.
Echoes whisper tales of old,
In the dark, their wonders unfold.

Crickets chirp their evening song,
In this moment, we belong.
The cool embrace of dusk's delight,
A sanctuary, pure and bright.

As the darkness gently grows,
The night reveals what daylight knows.
In the stillness, hearts take flight,
Linger here, 'neath the deepening night.

Whispers of Dusk

As daylight ebbs, the colors fade,
Soft hues wrap the earth like shade.
Whispers of dusk in gentle tones,
Embrace the world in twilight's bones.

A moment held, a breath of peace,
In the quiet, troubles cease.
Stars peek out, a shimmering lace,
In the dusky veil, we find our place.

Crimson skies give way to night,
Finding solace in their light.
Every leaf and petal sighs,
In the hush, the spirit flies.

As shadows blend with twilight's thread,
Painting dreams where hopes are fed.
In the whispers, we align,
With the magic of the divine.

Echoes of Twilight

In twilight's glow, the world does pause,
Reflecting on its fleeting cause.
Echoes linger in the air,
Stories told without a care.

The horizon blushes, shades align,
Nature's canvas, pure and fine.
Beneath the fading, soft embrace,
We find our thoughts in a sacred space.

Stars awaken, one by one,
As the day bows to the night begun.
A hush descends, peace takes flight,
In the beauty of the twilight.

Time stands still, a gentle sway,
Capturing moments, come what may.
In echoes soft, our hearts will sing,
Of love and life that twilight brings.

Ember's Last Dance

In the twilight, embers glow,
A final waltz, soft and slow.
Whispers in the fading light,
Hold onto warmth, bid goodnight.

The shadows stretch, the fire sighs,
A fleeting flame beneath the skies.
Echoes of laughter linger near,
As the stars begin to appear.

With every flicker, memories fade,
A tapestry of dreams displayed.
Yet in the dark, hope finds its way,
Guiding the heart through end of day.

As the last ember dances low,
We embrace the night's deep glow.
For in the silence, life renews,
The promise of dawn, soft and true.

Hues of Diminishing Calm

The skies bleed colors, soft and wan,
A canvas brushed by the serene dawn.
Whispers of winds through chased hues,
Draw the heart to love's sweet muse.

Azure mingles with shades of grey,
Each moment precious, fading away.
Golden rays kiss the earth goodbye,
As daylight bows, the night draws nigh.

Reflections dance on tranquil streams,
Shattering silence, weaving dreams.
Nature's hush cradles the soul,
In every twilight, we are whole.

In this serene, diminishing light,
We find our shadows, merge with night.
Letting go leads to rebirth,
In every ending, there's new worth.

Echoes of Dimming Radiance

As the sun dips low in the sky,
Echoes of daylight start to sigh.
Shadows creep where light has played,
In the twilight, memories swayed.

Time carries whispers, soft and light,
Trading warmth for the cool of night.
Each fading breath, a tale unfolds,
In the depths where silence holds.

Stars punctuate the velvet dark,
Hiding dreams like a secret spark.
In the distance, the moon peeks through,
Illuminating paths, old and new.

Yet in the quiet, a song remains,
Of love and loss, of joy and pains.
Though radiance wanes, spirits soar,
In echoes of light, we long for more.

Canvas of Dusk's Lament

A brush of dusk paints the sky,
With strokes of sorrow, drawing nigh.
Colors bleed, rich and deep,
A tender hush as shadows creep.

The day surrenders, yields to night,
In the stillness, finds respite.
Lament of sun's last, brilliant blaze,
Fades softly into twilight's haze.

Stars awaken, blinking bright,
Cradled in the arms of night.
Each glimmer tells a story old,
Of dreams lost and hearts bold.

In this canvas, time stands still,
Nature carries a soft thrill.
A dance of colors, deep and vast,
In dusk's lament, we weave the past.

Whispers of Dusk

As daylight fades to softly sigh,
The stars awaken in the sky.
A gentle hush wraps round the trees,
In twilight's arms, a tender breeze.

The river murmurs secrets low,
While shadows dance on earth below.
A symphony of night begins,
As tranquil peace the heart now wins.

The moon ascends, a silver queen,
In stillness found, a sacred scene.
The world exhales, no more to rush,
Embraced within the whispers' hush.

In dusk's embrace, our worries flee,
Each moment draped in mystery.
A quiet promise softly glows,
In whispers of the dusk that flows.

Last Gleam of Day

The sun dips low, a fiery hue,
Casting gold on skies so blue.
With every ray, a day's goodbye,
As fleeting moments softly lie.

The clouds ignite in colors bright,
A canvas painted; pure delight.
The world below shifts into shade,
As twilight's brush begins to fade.

Birds sing their final, sweet refrain,
As shadows stretch across the plain.
The last gleam of day bids farewell,
In tranquil tones, a magic spell.

With every dusk, a hope anew,
For dreams to bloom where skies are blue.
In the last light, we find our way,
Embracing night, we greet the day.

Shadows Embrace the End

A veil of night begins to weave,
In quiet corners, shadows cleave.
They reach and stretch, a soft caress,
Embracing all in their finesse.

The fading light, a gentle kiss,
In twilight's arms, we find our bliss.
Each whispered breath, each silent glance,
Invites us forth in night's soft dance.

The stars align, their paths unseen,
While shadows linger, calm and keen.
They cradle hearts and guide the way,
As night unfolds the dreams we sway.

In shadows deep, we find the end,
A sweet surrender, time to mend.
For in the dark, the promise grows,
As shadows grasp the quiet throes.

Twilight's Gentle Farewell

The sky ablaze with colors grand,
As twilight calls with beckoning hand.
Each brushstroke spreads a fading light,
Preparing hearts for soothing night.

The stars emerge, a twinkling glow,
A tapestry that starts to show.
With every sparkle, dreams ignite,
As shadows wink and grant us flight.

The day retreats, its whispers low,
In twilight's cloak, we come to know.
A time to pause, a chance to breathe,
In twilight's grace, we gently weave.

In every hush, a story told,
Of love and life in colors bold.
As night descends, with softest bell,
We bid adieu, twilight's farewell.

The Quiet Exodus

In whispers soft, the shadows creep,
A silent march, where secrets seep.
The fading light, a gentle sigh,
As dreams take flight, beneath the sky.

Among the trees, the echoes fade,
A path once bright, now softly laid.
With every step, the past unspools,
In twilight's hush, we find our jewels.

Memories dance like fireflies,
In twilight's glow, they pierce the skies.
We leave behind what once was dear,
In the quiet night, we shed our fear.

With every heartbeat, we renew,
The strength that lies in hearts so true.
The journey long, yet we embrace,
The quiet exodus, our sacred space.

Night's Gentle Ascent

The stars emerge, a silver dance,
As moonlight weaves its soft expanse.
The earth transforms beneath the night,
In shadows deep, we find our light.

With every breath, a lullaby,
That whispers softly from the sky.
The world adorned in velvet hues,
A tranquil pause, as time renews.

In sighs and dreams, both near and far,
The heart ignites like a distant star.
In silence wrapped, we drift away,
Night's gentle ascent, our sweet ballet.

Each hidden path, a tale untold,
In starlit night, the brave and bold.
So let us wander, hand in hand,
Through night's embrace, a promised land.

Stray Luminescence

Amidst the dark, a flicker glows,
A spark of hope, where courage grows.
In shadows cast by fears unsealed,
A stray luminescence revealed.

In quiet corners, life persists,
A dance of light with gentle twists.
Each glimmer found, a story shone,
In every heart, not left alone.

As shadows play upon the wall,
A hidden guide that hears our call.
Through tangled paths, the light will lead,
To brighter days where dreams will breed.

So let us cherish each small spark,
For in the night, it lights the dark.
With every glow, we'll find our way,
Embrace the dawn of a new day.

Eclipsing Beauty

A moment still, the sun gives way,
As shadows chase the light of day.
In quiet awe, the world convenes,
To witness grace in twilight scenes.

With every heartbeat, time suspends,
An eclipse whispers, beauty bends.
The colors merge, a deep embrace,
In nature's art, we find our place.

The sky adorned with shades divine,
As light retreats, yet we still shine.
In darkness, hope begins to weave,
A tapestry that we believe.

So let us linger, gaze in awe,
At fleeting moments that we draw.
For in the shadows, love can grow,
Eclipsing beauty, a wondrous glow.

In the Wake of Dusk

The shadows stretch and grow,
As daylight bids goodbye,
Whispers of the night begin,
Underneath the twilight sky.

Stars awaken one by one,
To dance on velvet seas,
Moonlight drapes the earth in silver,
Carried by the gentle breeze.

Crickets sing their evening song,
While fireflies weave through air,
Nature holds its breath in peace,
As night assumes its care.

Time softens in this hour,
Where dreams are born anew,
In the wake of dusk we find,
A world bathed in deep blue.

Glorious Decline

Autumn leaves, a fiery show,
Upon the ground they lie,
A golden dance of letting go,
Beneath the fading sky.

The trees stand bare, yet strong,
Their branches reach for light,
In every end, beginnings bloom,
In shadows, hope takes flight.

The sun, triumphant in its flight,
Descends with grace so fine,
Each day a step towards the night,
In glorious decline.

Yet in this quiet surrender,
Life finds a way to thrive,
In every moment soft and tender,
The spirit remains alive.

The Dimming Canvas

Brush strokes fade into the eve,
As colors start to blend,
A masterpiece of light recedes,
And gives in to the end.

Hues of pink and gold dissolve,
In twilight's gentle grasp,
The canvas dims, as shadows weave,
Their cool embrace to clasp.

The stars pierce through, a sparkling thread,
On dark fabric, they gleam,
A silent song, the night has spread,
Where dreams begin to dream.

In this soft, embracing dusk,
Life's palette finds its way,
The world asleep, in tranquil husk,
Awaiting a new day.

Epilogue of the Day

The sun dips low, a final bow,
Casting shadows long,
Day whispers soft its sweet farewell,
In twilight's tender song.

Stars prepare their nightly stage,
As blue steals over gold,
Each moment laced with quiet grace,
A story yet untold.

The moon ascends, a silver disk,
To guard the world asleep,
In every sigh, in every breath,
The mysteries we keep.

This epilogue, a gentle breeze,
Carries dreams on high,
In the stillness, hearts find peace,
As day says its goodbye.

Crafting the Dark

In shadows deep, we weave our tales,
What once was light, now softly pales.
With whispers low, the night awakes,
As moonlight dances on silent lakes.

Each brush of dusk, a hidden art,
Where secrets linger, hearts depart.
A tapestry of fears and dreams,
Crafted in silence, or so it seems.

The stars conspire in their own song,
Reminding us where we belong.
In every corner, stories hide,
The dark, a canvas, vast and wide.

In quiet moments, truths are forged,
As starlit visions are poured and gorged.
In shadows deep, we find our spark,
Art lives anew, crafting the dark.

Whispers of a Dimming Day

The sun dips low, a gentle sigh,
Painting the sky in twilight's cry.
Beneath the hush, the world holds still,
As darkness drapes, a tender thrill.

In fading light, the birds take flight,
Seeking shadows in the coming night.
The trees stand tall, in silence they sway,
Embracing whispers of a dimming day.

Petals close, their colors fade,
As twilight's calm begins to invade.
The air is thick with secrets shared,
With every breath, we are ensnared.

A soft farewell, the daylight wanes,
In echoes faint, the evening reigns.
In shadows cast, our hopes will play,
In whispered dreams of a dimming day.

The Color of Silence

In quietude, a hue unfolds,
A palette pure, no tales retold.
The gentle gray, the softest blue,
A space where thoughts find form anew.

Each moment paused, a breath of peace,
In tranquil stillness, worries cease.
The whispers dance, though none can hear,
In colors muted, calm and clear.

The world a canvas, vast and wide,
Where shades of silence tenderly hide.
In every space, the echoes lay,
The depth, the truth, the color of gray.

Listen closely, let stillness reign,
In each soft shade, the heart's refrain.
In quiet whispers, we find our way,
In the color of silence, we choose to stay.

Light's Last Embrace

As daylight fades, we feel the pull,
Of shadows gathering, soft and full.
In twilight's glow, a promise lies,
As stars awaken in velvet skies.

The sun bids peace, its journey ends,
While dusk descends, the night descends.
In whispered tones, the world exhales,
Light's last embrace in gentle trails.

The fireflies spark, a fleeting dance,
In softest glimmers, they take their chance.
Within the dark, our dreams expand,
Caressed by night's all-knowing hand.

With every breath, a story starts,
In echo's hush, we mend our hearts.
In radiant shadows, love interlaces,
In the stillness of light's last embraces.

Fading Echoes of Brilliance

In shadows cast by brightened skies,
The spark of light begins to pale.
Whispers of dreams in twilight rise,
As time unwinds its fragile tale.

Fading soft, the colors blend,
A canvas wrapped in silken thread.
Moments linger, only to bend,
To memories where once we fled.

A tune that echoes, faint and clear,
Pulsing through the heart of night.
Yet deeply felt, the threads we wear,
In shimmering dark, they hold their light.

So let the soft and hushed refrain,
Remind us what once filled the air.
For in the stillness, we remain,
In fading echoes, always there.

The Hour Before Darkness

A quiet hush before the fall,
The world awaits in muted breath.
Each heartbeat echoes nature's call,
Entwined with whispers, life and death.

The sun dips low, a golden arc,
Painting shadows on the ground.
In this brief glow, we face the stark,
Anticipation's lingering sound.

Moments stretch, as glances meet,
A fleeting dance of silent grace.
In twilight's grasp, our hearts feel sweet,
In shadows cast, we find our place.

Before the dark claims the day,
We hold the light, a fragile prize.
In this soft hour, we will stay,
And watch the stars embrace the skies.

Fragments of Dimming Dawn

As morning breaks, the light is torn,
Through veils of mist and shadowed streams.
The world awakes, yet still forlorn,
In fragments woven from our dreams.

The sky, a canvas smeared with hues,
Pastels and grays fight to ignite.
Yet in this dance of fading blues,
We glimpse the birth of morning light.

A fleeting calm cloaks the sight,
Where whispers swirl and silence sighs.
In broken shards, the day takes flight,
As night's embrace reluctantly flies.

With every breath, we touch the core,
Of fleeting time, forever drawn.
In scattered pieces, we explore,
The beauty found in dimming dawn.

A Dance with No Sun

In the absence of golden rays,
Shadows sway in graceful arcs.
Underneath the moon's embrace,
We twirl amid the chilly sparks.

With every move, the night unfolds,
A symphony only stars can play.
In whispers soft, the story told,
Of dreams that linger, drift away.

Each step we take, a breath of loss,
Yet in the dark, new hopes ignite.
This dance, though cold, bears not a cross,
For in the void, we find our light.

So let us sway, though sun will fade,
With moonlit hearts, we find our way.
In shadows deep, a choice is made,
To celebrate this night's ballet.

Faint Illumination

In twilight's grasp, shadows linger,
A whispering breeze starts to sing,
Stars appear, a distant glimmer,
Night unfolds her velvet wing.

Moonlight dances on the leaves,
Awakening secrets from the past,
Gentle echoes weave through trees,
Faint illumination, shadows cast.

The world slows down, time suspends,
A tranquil heart begins to soar,
Waves of silence, nature bends,
In this moment, we want more.

Through the dusk, a promise shines,
Each flicker speaks without a sound,
A soft embrace of tangled vines,
In faint illumination, we are found.

Subtle Farewell

As twilight fades, I bid adieu,
The day retreats with quiet grace,
A lingering touch, a gentle hue,
In soft goodbyes, emotions trace.

Voices dim, the laughter wanes,
Empty echoes fill the air,
Each memory like distant trains,
Softly fading, unaware.

A turning page, a fleeting glance,
The final bow, the curtain falls,
Yet in the silence, dreams still dance,
In subtle farewell, love calls.

The stars emerge as night draws near,
Carrying whispers from the past,
In every heartbeat, I hold dear,
Though we part, our bond will last.

Softening Horizons

When dawn breaks through the night's embrace,
A canvas painted in gold and rose,
The horizon softens, time finds space,
In gentle whispers, the new day grows.

Clouds drift lazily in the sky,
Reflecting colors, warm and kind,
The chill retreats, a heartfelt sigh,
In the softening, peace we find.

Birds awaken, their songs ignite,
Nature stirs from slumber's call,
As light envelops, wrongs turn right,
Softening horizons embrace us all.

With each sunrise, hope is reborn,
In tender light, the world anew,
The beauty of a day not worn,
In softening horizons, dreams come true.

Gradual Disappearance

Like fading echoes in the night,
Moments drift away with grace,
Softly swallowed by the light,
In gradual disappearance, time takes its place.

Memories linger, yet grow thin,
As shadows stretch and colors blend,
An empty space where love had been,
Filling heartbeats that slowly end.

The dust of ages weighs so light,
On weary souls that chose to stay,
In the tranquil dance of endless night,
We find in loss the strength to play.

Yet in the fading, hope remains,
Emerging where the darkness tips,
In gradual disappearance, change sustains,
A hint of light in whispered slips.

Shadows Paint the Sky

Shadows stretch across the ground,
As the sun begins to dip.
Colors swirl, then fade away,
A fleeting, magic trip.

Night creeps in with velvet grace,
Stars awaken, one by one.
Whispers of the evening breeze,
As daylight's dreams are done.

Figures dance in twilight glow,
Mysteries start to bloom.
Every shadow seems to speak,
In the gathering gloom.

Hope lingers in the dark,
Yet darkness has its charm.
In stillness, a heart will find,
Comfort beneath its calm.

Whispering Colors

In the garden, colors play,
Whispering secrets soft and low.
Petals flutter with each breeze,
Telling tales only they know.

Sunlight dances on the leaves,
Painting shadows on the ground.
Nature's canvas, rich and warm,
In its beauty, peace is found.

The sky dons a cloak of hue,
Brushing clouds with shades of dreams.
Every moment, life ignites,
In a symphony of beams.

With each sunset, colors blend,
A masterpiece, bold and bright.
In this world of wonder's hand,
The heart learns to take flight.

Gentle Erosion of Light

The day recedes, a soft goodbye,
As shadows weave their silky thread.
A whisper fades, an echo sighs,
Where brilliant warmth once gently spread.

Fingers of dusk brush the trees,
As twilight weaves a silver veil.
Each moment slips, a fading breeze,
In the silence, a fragile tale.

Stars emerge like scattered dreams,
In the vast expanse, they gleam.
The world wrapped tight in night's embrace,
Reminds us life is but a stream.

Time drifts on like sand in glass,
Moments lost to endless flight.
Yet in the still, a promise cast,
Of dawn that breaks the softest night.

Fading into Silence

In the quiet, voices cease,
Softly fades the world away.
Nature hushes, finding peace,
In the twilight's gentle sway.

Leaves whisper to the setting sun,
As shadows dance on forest floors.
The day's chorus now is done,
Echoes linger, then withdraw.

Stars arrive with a silent grace,
Cradling dreams from daytime's wane.
In their glow, a sacred space,
Where hopes and fears can wane.

Embrace the still, let go of noise,
Find the calm that lingers near.
In the darkness, hear your voice,
Fading softly, disappear.

Lingering Shadows

In the dusk where whispers play,
Shadows dance, softly sway.
Echoes of a day long spent,
Memories in silence lent.

Beneath the tree, a secret's kept,
Within the night, the dreamers slept.
Fingers trace the fading light,
In the stillness of the night.

Footsteps fade on trails of dark,
While hidden sparks ignite a spark.
Lingering thoughts, they intertwine,
In the heart where shadows shine.

As the night begins to weave,
In the hush, we dare believe.
Shadows linger, soft and long,
In the depths where we belong.

Surrendering Radiance

Golden rays break through the gray,
Illuminating life's ballet.
Flowers bloom with vibrant cheer,
Each petal whispers, "I am here."

Sunset paints the sky anew,
Crimson hues that kiss the blue.
Embrace the warmth, let it flow,
Surrender to the radiant glow.

Moments lost in fleeting time,
Echoes hum a tender rhyme.
With every breath, we rise and fall,
And find our place within it all.

In the calm, let shadows flee,
Awakening the soul to see.
Surrendering to light's embrace,
We find our peace, our hidden grace.

Twilight's Breath

As twilight whispers soft goodbyes,
The stars emerge to fill the skies.
Cool winds weave through the trees,
Carrying secrets with gentle pleas.

The horizon shades of gray and gold,
Stories of the day retold.
Shadows stretch, embracing night,
In twilight's breath, we feel the light.

Crickets sing their evening song,
While the world finds where it belongs.
With every sigh, the day exhales,
In this stillness, beauty prevails.

In the calm of dusk's caress,
We navigate through thoughtfulness.
Twilight's breath, a sacred space,
A fleeting glimpse of time's embrace.

Hushed Glow

In the quiet where shadows meet,
A soft glow dances, bittersweet.
Stars blink softly in twilight's kiss,
Every moment a fleeting bliss.

The moon hangs low, a watchful eye,
Guarding dreams that linger nigh.
Each heartbeat whispers, tender and slow,
In the stillness, a hushed glow.

Whispers of love drift through the air,
Entwined in silence, beyond compare.
Caressed by night, our spirits soar,
With every breath, we are forevermore.

In this peace, our souls ignite,
Illuminated by the gentle light.
Hushed glow in the dark, our guide,
Hand in hand, forever side by side.

Faint Radiance of Solitude

In the quiet of the night,
Whispers drift on gentle dreams,
Stars blink soft, a distant light,
Embracing all that silence seems.

Lonely paths where shadows tread,
Murmurs of the heart remain,
A tapestry of thoughts unsaid,
Woven softly with joy and pain.

Moonbeams dance on empty streets,
Casting silver on my skin,
A delicate world that retreats,
Into the depth where hopes begin.

In solitude, I find my song,
A melody of tranquil air,
Each note a place where I belong,
In faint radiance lingering there.

Glimmers in the Dusk

As twilight spills its velvet hue,
Fleeting moments brush the sky,
Soft glimmers calling out anew,
Where day and night gently lie.

The horizon blurs in muted grace,
With hints of gold that hold the gaze,
In every shadow, a new embrace,
A dance of light through evening's maze.

Whispers rustle in the leaves,
Secrets shared as shadows creep,
In the heart, a hope believes,
That dreams are born from twilight's sleep.

Each glimmer holds a fleeting chance,
To capture moments, bright yet brief,
As dusk invites the night's first dance,
And guides us to our own belief.

When Colors Turn to Grey

Upon the canvas, shades dissolve,
As vibrant hues begin to fade,
Where once were dreams, now lost resolve,
A memory of light, delayed.

The world transforms in quiet sighs,
A palette turned to muted tones,
Each echo of the past complies,
In whispers soft as quiet stones.

Yet in this grey, a strength remains,
A balance found in less defined,
In shadows deep, resilience gains,
A truth more complex, intertwined.

So when the colors drift away,
We learn to see with softened light,
In varied shades both night and day,
New visions spark from quiet night.

Evening's Soft Descent

When day gives way to night's embrace,
The sun dips low, a gentle sigh,
With tender hues that softly trace,
The edge of earth and velvet sky.

A hush envelops all around,
As stars awaken, shy and bright,
In silence, whispers weave profound,
Creating calm in fading light.

The world holds breath in twilight's grace,
A moment where all fears subside,
In every heart, a sacred space,
As evening's beauty turns the tide.

With each descent, a promise kept,
That dreams await in shaded glow,
In evening's arms, the heart has leapt,
To find the peace where shadows flow.

Evaporating Dreams

In the quiet of night, they take flight,
Whispers of hopes, fading from sight.
Like shadows at dawn, they wane away,
Longing to linger, yet led astray.

Fleeting and fragile, like dew on grass,
Moments diminish, too swift to amass.
Each wish a whisper, a sigh in the breeze,
Stirring the heart, but never to seize.

Figures once vivid, now dimmed in the mist,
Holding on tight to the ones that were missed.
Chasing the echoes, lost in the stream,
Awake in the dawning, of evaporating dreams.

Fade into silence, where hopes once gleamed,
Into the vastness, where nothing redeemed.
But still, we wander, with hearts full of light,
Searching for dreams in the depths of the night.

Nocturnal Embrace

Wrapped in the shadows, where secrets lie,
The moon whispers softly, a tender sigh.
Stars flicker gently, a song from afar,
In this nocturnal embrace, we are who we are.

With silence as music, the world feels light,
Dreams weave like ribbons through the fabric of night.
Each twinkling star a guardian's glance,
Lost in the magic, we sway in a dance.

Beneath velvet skies, where solace appears,
Hand in hand, we conquer our fears.
The night is alive, pulsing like a heart,
A tapestry woven, from whispers to art.

In this stillness, we find our place,
Lost in the wonder of the night's warm embrace.
Together we wander, till dawn's gentle beam,
Hand in hand forever, lost in a dream.

The Final Flicker

A candle burns low, whispers of grace,
In shadows it dances, with time to embrace.
Flickering gently, the light starts to sway,
Memories linger, then fade away.

The dusk calls us closer, a silent retreat,
When warmth turns to silence, and echoes defeat.
Yet in that moment, still flickers a flame,
Holding a promise that life is the same.

In twilight's soft grasp, we gather our fear,
Each heartbeat a rhythm, each sigh a tear.
Through the shadows of evening, we search for the spark,

Guided by embers that light up the dark.

As the last glow dims, and daylight breaks in,
We hold onto hope, for a new day to begin.
For in every ending, a flicker remains,
A promise of life, where love still sustains.

Emptiness of Light

In the glow of the evening, shadows align,
Chasing the echoes where bright colors twine.
Yet beneath the surface, a stillness takes flight,
A haunting reminder of emptiness light.

Radiant glimmers, once vibrant and bold,
Now whisper of stories too fragile to hold.
In the spaces between, a void softly calls,
Emptiness lingers, where wonder once sprawled.

Glimpse into twilight, where silence reigns king,
Each flicker a memory, a sorrow we bring.
Longing for brilliance, in shadows we dwell,
Searching for solace, in this fragile shell.

Yet in the absence, a beauty does lie,
In the stillness of night, with a darkened sky.
For light's emptiness teaches us to feel,
In the depths of the quiet, our hearts can heal.

Lullaby of the Setting Sun

Whispers of dusk caress the sky,
Colors blend as shadows sigh.
Waves of warmth in twilight flow,
Cradled gently, dreams will grow.

Stars emerge from slumber's call,
Night's embrace will cover all.
Crickets sing a soft refrain,
Lullabies of light and pain.

The horizon dips, a final bow,
Time to rest, the sun knows how.
In this hush, the world will sleep,
Guardian of secrets we keep.

Crimson fades to deep indigo,
In the night, sweet visions glow.
Beneath the veil of starlit hue,
Endless dreams await us too.

Transient Brilliance

Moments shine like fleeting sparks,
Illuminating hidden marks.
In the heart's embrace they dwell,
Stories told but hard to tell.

Glimmers dance on evening's edge,
Fragile dreams that softly hedge.
With each breath, they fade away,
Leaving echoes of the day.

Time flows like a gentle stream,
We chase the light, we chase the dream.
But in the shadows, truth resides,
In silence where our hope abides.

Hold these moments, soft and bright,
In your hands, let them ignite.
For though they slip through our embrace,
Their essence lingers, leaves a trace.

Fading Radiance

Once ablaze, now soft and pale,
Memories wrapped in a gentle veil.
The sun dips low, its final bow,
Breath of twilight, here and now.

Whispers linger like distant chimes,
Fading echoes of olden times.
Within the dusk, the shadows play,
Holding tight to the end of day.

Each glimmer holds a tale untold,
The warmth of moments, a gentle mold.
As light retreats, the night draws near,
Its tender hush can calm the fear.

In the waning glow, we find our peace,
With every heartbeat, sweet release.
Embrace the night, let worries cease,
For in the dark, our souls increase.

The Twilight Serenade

Between the day and night we stand,
Golden hues stretch out their hand.
A serenade of soft goodbyes,
In the sky, where silence flies.

Melodies drift on zephyrs' wing,
With every note, the darkness sings.
Starry whispers fill the air,
Enchanting hearts with tender care.

The horizon blurs, where dreams take flight,
In twilight's grasp, everything's right.
Hold this moment, let it stay,
Wrapped in warmth, we'll find our way.

As shadows deepen, echoes blend,
A song of dusk that has no end.
In twilight's arms, we'll softly sway,
Cradled gently until the break of day.